# not a guide to

# Wirral

## Dan Longman

First published 2013

The History Press
The Mill, Brimscombe Port
Stroud, Gloucestershire, GL5 2QG
www.thehistorypress.co.uk

British Library Cataloguing in Publication Data.
A catalogue record for this book is available from the British Library.

ISBN 978 0 7524 9919 2

Typesetting and origination by The History Press
Printed in Great Britain

# Coat of Arms

BY FAITH AND FORESIGHT

The design symbolises the Wirral Peninsula which was founded as a borough in 1972. The central charge is a trident taken from the existing crest of Wallasey denoting the diverse maritime traits of the area. Suspended from this is a conventionalised representation of the Wirral Horn reflecting the ancient tenure of the Forest of Wirral by cornage. This was an early form of land tenure which obliged the tenant to give notice of an invasion by blowing a horn.

\*

Above the shield is the closed helm with a twisted crest-wreath and decorative mantling in green and gold characterizing the rural parts of the Wirral and the sands of the coast. On a sandstone rock representing Hilbre Island sits an oystercatcher from Hoylake's crest. Flanking this are two sprigs of the Bog Myrtle, typical of the area, all enclosed within a gold 'palisado' crown. These five points indicate the five areas of the borough.

\*

On the left is the lion of Randle Meschines, Third Earl of Chester, who formed the entire Hundred of Wirral into a Forest administered by the Master Foresters from Storeton. The crosier in the lion's paw represents St Werburgh's Abbey at Chester.

\*

The motto, 'By Faith and Foresight', is inspired by words in the mottoes of Birkenhead (Fides - 'Faith') and Hoylake (Prospice - 'Look ahead').

# Contents

| | |
|---|---|
| Wirral | 6 |
| Grid Reference | 8 |
| Street Names | 10 |
| Timeline | 12 |
| Distance From | 14 |
| My Wirral | 16 |
| A Day in the Life | 20 |
| Freak Weather | 22 |
| A Storm at New Brighton | 24 |
| How Many Times a Year | 26 |
| Demographics | 28 |
| Strange Statistics | 30 |
| Quotations Through History | 34 |
| Famous For | 38 |
| Infamous For | 44 |
| Wirral in Days Gone By: Landing Stage, Woodside | 46 |
| Making the Headlines | 48 |
| Letters to The Press | 52 |
| Rebellious Wirral | 56 |
| Buildings: the Best | 60 |

Buildings: the Worst                                        64
Historic Miscellany                                        66
Museums and Galleries                                      70
Parks and Green Spaces                                     72
Businesses                                                 74
Political Figures                                          78
Wirral Firsts                                              82
Victorian Wirral                                           84
Crime and the Macabre                                      86
Ghosts                                                     90
Wirral at War                                              92
Notable Residents                                          94
Festivals                                                 104
Wirral in Days Gone By: Hamilton Square, Birkenhead       108
Musicians                                                 110
Local Lingo                                               114
Wirral on Screen                                          116
Future Wirral                                             120
Websites                                                  122
Things to do in Wirral                                    124
Picture Credits                                           126

# Wirral

The name Wirral appears in the Anglo-Saxon Chronicle as Wirheal, literally meaning 'myrtle corner'. The Old English *wir*, meant a myrtle tree, with *heal* meaning an angle or corner. It is supposed that the peninsula was once overgrown with bog myrtle, a plant no longer found here but plentiful in nearby Formby which Wirral would once have resembled. The name was given to the Hundred of Wirral around the eighth century.

# Merseyrail

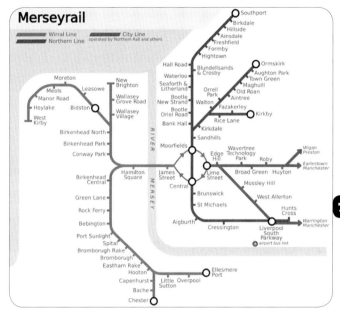

Wirral Line
Northern Line
City Line
operated by Northern Rail and others

Southport
Birkdale
Hillside
Ainsdale
Freshfield
Formby
Hightown

Moreton
Leasowe
New Brighton
Meols
Manor Road
Hoylake
Bidston
Wallasey Grove Road
Wallasey Village
West Kirby

Hall Road
Blundellsands & Crosby
Waterloo
Seaforth & Litherland
Bootle New Strand
Bootle Oriel Road
Bank Hall

Ormskirk
Aughton Park
Town Green
Maghull
Orrell Park
Old Roan
Walton
Aintree
Fazakerley
Rice Lane
Kirkby

Kirkdale
Sandhills

Birkenhead North
Birkenhead Park
Conway Park

Moorfields

Wavertree Technology Park
Edge Hill
Roby
Broad Green
Huyton

Wigan
Preston

Earlestown
Manchester

Hamilton Square
James Street
Central
Lime Street
Mossley Hill
West Allerton

Birkenhead Central
Green Lane
Rock Ferry
Bebington
Port Sunlight
Spital
Bromborough Rake
Bromborough
Eastham Rake
Hooton
Capenhurst
Bache
Chester

Brunswick
St Michaels
Aigburth
Cressington
Liverpool South Parkway
Hunts Cross

Warrington
Manchester

airport bus link

Little Sutton
Overpool
Ellesmere Port

RIVER MERSEY

# Grid Reference

53° 19′ 21.62″ N, 3° 2′ 49.57″ W

# Street Names

The ancient landscape of Wirral features numerous towns and villages, each of which have grown and evolved over many centuries. However, their population levels rocketed in the nineteenth century and it was in this period that many of the streets and roads we recognise today began to take shape.

Some of the more interesting road names include Birkenhead's assortment of arboreal streets. This includes Lowwood Road, Cedar Street and Maple Street which pay homage to the town's title. It is believed that the name Birkenhead comes from the Old English description of the headland with the birch trees, with plenty of forest and woodland still in existence at the time of the town's early development. In Bebington you will find several Shakespearian connections epitomised through addresses such as Juliet Avenue, named after the famous love-struck character of Juliet. Not far from here stands Miranda Avenue named after the beautiful daughter of Duke Prospero in *The Tempest*, as well as Rosalind Avenue, from the play *As You Like It*. Up in Bidston Village is the very quaint School Lane. This route once led to an old schoolhouse dating from near the outbreak of the English Civil War. It was later replaced in the Victorian era but destroyed during the Blitz. In Hoylake is the rather regal Kings Gap, so-called after King William III. In 1690 the monarch set sail from here with 10,000 men to do battle with James II. He went on to claim victory in what became known as the Battle of the Boyne. Heswall's elevated position gives credence to the origin of the town's Dee View Road, the Dee being a 70-mile-long river flowing down from the Welsh mountains of Snowdonia.

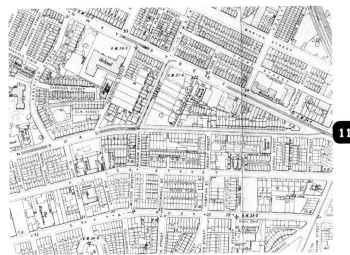

# Timeline

Edward III grants a charter to the Priory and its successors to provide a ferry service to passengers.

James Atherton purchases the sand hills that will become the seaside resort of New Brighton.

The Battle of Brunanburh takes place in Bebington.

Flint tools suggest early human activity in Wirral from this period.

Earl Ranulph le Meschin converts much of Wirral into a large hunting forest.

A diversion in the river Dee to improve access to Chester accelerates the silting up of the West Wirral shore.

| 7000 BC | 937 | 1120 | 1330 | 1737 | 1830 |
|---------|-----|------|------|------|------|
| | 902 | 1086 | 1150 | 1690 | 1824 |

Vikings settle on the peninsula founding places such as Thingwall, Frankby and Meols.

Birkenhead Priory established by Hamon de Masci for the Order of Saint Benedict.

William Laird establishes his business at Wallasey Pool and lays out exciting plans for Birkenhead.

The Domesday Book reveals Wirral is one of the most densely populated areas in the land, with Eastham Manor being the second largest in Cheshire.

King William III sails from Hoylake on his military expedition to Ireland.

An Act of Parliament brings the Birkenhead and Liverpool docks under the single ownership of the Mersey Docks and Harbour Company.

The Third World Scout Jamboree is held at Arrowe Park.

Birkenhead Park is completed to Joseph Paxton's grand vision.

The Mersey Railway tunnel considerably cuts cross-river journey times.

Bombs rain down on Wirral as the German Luftwaffe launches its first attacks.

**1847**   **1857**   **1886**   **1929**   **1940**

**1840**   **1853**   **1860**   **1888**   **1934**   **1974**

Price's Patent Candle Company purchases land at Bromborough Pool to house its workers.

William Lever establishes the village of Port Sunlight for soap manufacturing.

The Metropolitan Borough of Wirral incorporated.

George Stephenson designs a rail track linking Wirral to Chester.

George F. Train opens the first street railway in Europe to run in Birkenhead.

The Queensway Tunnel is opened by King George V.

# Distance From

| Place | Km | Miles |
|---|---|---|
| Angkor Wat, Cambodia | 10,135 | 6,298 |
| Brussels, Belgium | 578 | 359 |
| Cairo Citadel, Egypt | 3,796 | 2,359 |
| Death Valley, USA | 8,130 | 5,052 |
| Eiffel Tower, France | 630 | 392 |
| Frankfurt, Germany | 882 | 548 |
| Gateshead Millennium Bridge, Newcastle | 196 | 122 |
| Hong Kong, China | 9,687 | 6,019 |
| Istanbul, Turkey | 2,752 | 1,710 |
| Jerusalem, Israel | 3,876 | 2,409 |
| The Kremlin, Russia | 2,601 | 1,616 |
| London, England | 290 | 180 |
| Mana Pools, Zimbabwe | 8,541 | 5,308 |
| Niagara Falls, North America | 5,484 | 3,408 |
| Osaka, Japan | 9,459 | 5,878 |
| Palermo, Italy | 2,110 | 1,311 |
| Queenstown, New Zealand | 18,897 | 11,743 |
| Reykjavik, Iceland | 1,609 | 1,000 |
| Sandefjord, Norway | 1,034 | 643 |
| The Taj Mahal, India | 7,051 | 4,382 |
| Ural Mountains, Russia | 4,189 | 2,603 |
| Vatican City | 1,721 | 1,069 |
| Washington DC, USA | 5,666 | 3,521 |
| Xinyang, China | 8,762 | 5,445 |
| Yangambi, DR Congo | 6,622 | 4,115 |
| Zacatecas, Mexico | 8,808 | 5,474 |

# My Wirral

'Getting the tunnel bus home after a big night out is an education in itself. It's certainly something that everyone should experience.'

**Anne-Marie Almond, Registrar**

'What I love about the Wirral is being so close to the coast. I love that you can walk or cycle from Seacombe to Hooton, virtually without any contact with road traffic. We are so close to other places too: Manchester, Wales and even the Lakes are not too far away.'

**Joanne McAlpine, Service Manager**

'Whilst I welcome new retail developments for the employment opportunities and tourists it brings, I am saddened at the loss of those individual quirky retailers that made the towns and villages in Wirral so interesting.'

**Jane Owens, Administrator**

'I love living in Wirral. It's far nicer than big cities like London.'

**Mark Minshall, Fireman**

'Living here is great for the computer-lit, stay-at-home hermit types. The combination of bus limitations and naive Scouse friends means I can always create a perfect excuse to return. "The Mersey tunnel closes at 8pm! I need to get home!" They always believe it.'

**Simon Patrick Gabriel, Digital Marketer**

'I was privileged enough to have spent my childhood in New Ferry; a place which had a bypass built in order that it could be avoided. It's funny to hear people in Liverpool refer to Wirral as the 'posh side of the Mersey'.'

**Ben Montgomery, Student**

'There are far too many women with children that believe it's ok to pick kids up from school in their pyjamas.'

**Jenny Paton, Community Support Manager**

'Whether you live in a low socio-economic area or a neighbourhood more prosperous, quality education in Wirral is very inclusive. There are plenty of fantastic schools here offering pupils from all backgrounds a real opportunity to succeed in life.'

**Stephanie Batey, Teacher**

'Wirral is at the heart of an important area of natural beauty. It is difficult to imagine a more inviting place to live.'

**Nigel Green, President of the Liverpool Athenaeum**

'As a child living in Wirral I would always have great days out at New Brighton. The beach was lovely and we had some fantastic funfairs. It's not the same anymore but it's still a lovely place to visit.'

**Sheila O'Shea, Retired Carer**

'I love the way this peninsula contains so much variety, especially in its history. Within half an hour's walk of my house I can visit an old Roman quarry, a world-famous shipyard, a beautiful industrial village and the remains of a medieval priory.'

**Neil Holmes, Author**

# A Day in the Life

**06:00**   The morning sun rises over the glorious urban vista of the river Mersey.

**08:00**   Players at Tranmere Rovers prepare for another important match at their ground, Prenton Park.

**10:00**   Locals begin to flock to the Grange and Pyramids precinct for a busy day of shopping.

**12:00**   Diners sit down at Parkgate's Boathouse pub for a fine meal and a gorgeous view of North Wales.

**14:00**   Tourists explore the historic Victorian village of Port Sunlight and discover its industrious soap-making past.

**16:00**   Sleepy students leave their desks at Wirral Metropolitan College after a hard day of study.

**18:00**   Merseystravel transports passengers across the peninsula as rush hour reaches its peak.

**20:00**   Peckish filmgoers tuck into their popcorn at the Light Cinema in New Brighton.

**22:00**   Party-goers populate the trendy bars of West Kirby as their night out gets underway.

# Freak Weather

On 5 October 1832 an extraordinary tornado formed in Birkenhead. Back then there stood a pleasant dingle close to where William Laird had acquired land for his industrial expansion plans.

The clouds were said to be unusually low, appearing to actually touch the tops of trees, and there was a torrent of heavy rainfall. Without warning the wind increased violently and branches several feet thick were wrenched free from their bark and blown distances of up to 100 yards. Smaller shrubs were uprooted altogether and carried off out of sight. A man who had taken shelter by a wall was killed when it was blown down on top of him, whilst two others were fiercely pushed around by nature's force. A woman who had placed a large tub outside her cottage to collect rainwater was dismayed to see it rise from the ground and whirled off into the distance.

In January 1863, a terrible storm swept across the region. The heavy rain caused severe flooding and Wirral was no exception. A number of men employed on the Hooton to Ellesmere railway had noticed several rabbits and hares caught out by the adverse weather, taking refuge on a piece of land which had since become surrounded by water. Seeing the gastronomical opportunity before them, two of the labourers waded into the water and under heavy rain, struggled onwards towards the island. Upon reaching their destination they found their return had been cut off by the still rising water. On attempting to swim back, one of the men drowned. His companion succeeded in swimming to a tree where he was forced to wait for five hours until he could be rescued.

In September 1875, worshippers at Heswall parish church became panic-stricken when a terrifying tempest broke out during divine service. An intense flash of lightning followed by a loud crash of thunder plunged the building into near darkness as nearly all but a few of the candles were extinguished. Some of the braver members of the congregation who hadn't run in terror discovered that John Heveran, who had been playing the harmonium, had been struck dead by the lightning with his fingers still at the keys.

# A Storm at New Brighton

# How Many Times a Year

**Does a vehicle travel through the Queensway Tunnel?**
12.8 million, equal to 35,000 a day

**Do people visit the Wirral Farmers Market?**
26, every second Saturday to purchase a wide array of fresh local produce

**Does a commuter pass through Conway Park train station?**
1,724,000

**Does a Stena Line vessel sail from Wirral en route to Belfast?**
668, twice a day with a reduced Monday service and holidays

**Do people see a show at New Brighton's Floral Pavilion?**
260,000

# Demographics

**Population**
319,800

**Male**
153,800

**Female**
166,000

**Ethnicity**
Christian: 70.4%

Buddhist: 0.3%

Hindu: 0.2%

Jewish: 0.1%

Muslim: 0.6%

Sikh: 0.4%

Other: 0.3%

No religion or not stated: 28.1%

**Youngest and Oldest**
Aged 0-4: 18,500

Aged 90 and over: 2,900

# Strange Statistics

### 35 tons
Each Mersey Ferry can carry this amount of fuel, burning 12 tons an hour. They could travel from Wirral to New York without needing to refuel.

### 15
The Wirral peninsula is roughly 15 miles long and 7 miles wide.

### 1611
The area's oldest pub is reputedly the Wheatsheaf in Raby, dating back to 1611.

### 11
Hoylake has hosted the Open Gold Championships this many times, with the event set to return again in 2014.

### 84
There are this many schools to be found across Wirral.

### 450
This number died on board HMS *Birkenhead* in 1845. The frigate ran into rocks on the outskirts of Cape Town. The evacuation cry of 'women and children' became known as the Birkenhead Drill.

### £160,855
This was the average price for a house in Wirral in 2011.

### 260 feet
The height of Caldy Hill. It is thought to be the highest point in the area.

## 14.6

The life-expectancy gap between rich and poor Wirral males. The disparity between rich and poor females is 9.5 years.

## 42.16 knots

The World Windsurfing speed record was set when windsurfer Dave White attained this speed at West Kirby Marine Lake in October 1991. He held the record for two years.

## 5,865

Wirral had a population of this figure in the year 1801.

## 4

Wirral boasts four out of the five recommended North West beaches named in the 2012 *Good Beach Guide*.

## AD 1000

An ancient carving of a 'Sun Goddess' can be found on Bidston Hill, supposedly facing the rising sun on Midsummer's Day. It is thought to have been carved by the Norse-Irish around the last millennium.

## 16,567

Tranmere Rover's football ground, Prenton Park, can seat this may spectators.

## 1763

Leasowe Lighthouse, built in this year, is the oldest brick-built lighthouse in the UK.

## 2*d*

The price to enter Eastham Ferry Gardens in the year 1907.

# Quotations Through History

'Wyrale begynnith lesse than a quarter of a mile of the very Cite self of Chester, and withyn two bow shottes of the suburbe without the northe gate...Al the shore grounde of Wyral apon de side ys highe bankid, but not very hilly grounde. And so go the bank of Wyrale on to the Birket on Mersey side.'

**John Leland, Itinery, c. 1537**

'Helbre in Cheshire ann lland lynge betwixt the river of Lerpole and Westchester, a place veary parlus if the enimie should pocesse, for a smale fortiffication with one hundrethe soldears wold stoppe our passage into Irelande, and also not be removed withoutr hir majesty's forces.'

**Sir Edward Stanley, Defence Report, 1588**

'Til we come to the North Western shore, lying upon the Vergivian or Irish Sea, where are situte the township, parish and church of Kirkby in Walley, or Walsey, a town which hath fair lands, and where lie those fair sands, or plains, upon the shore of the sea, which, for the fitness for the purpose, allure the gentlemen and others oft to appoint great matches and venture no small sums in trying the swiftness of their horses.'

**William Webb, King's Vale Royal, c. 1630**

'Here is a ferry over the Mersee, which, at full sea, is more than two miles over. We land on the flat shore on the other side, and are contented to ride through the water for some length, not on horseback but on the shoulders of some honest Lancashire clown, who comes knee deep to the boat side, to truss you up, and then runs away with you, as nimbly as you desire to ride...'

**Daniel Defoe, A tour thro' the Whole Island of Great Britain, 1724-1726**

'It was a little, quiet grey village - so very grey, indeed, and venerable and quaint, that no flaunting red brick had dared to shew itself, and break the uniform tint of its gabled antiquity. The houses were grey, and the wall fences were grey and so was the church tower...And the old grange, with its mullioned windows and ivy-covered gateway, was the greyest of all.'

**Albert Smith describing Bidston in *The Struggles and Adventures of Christopher Tadpole*, 1848**

'Eastham is the finest old English village I have seen, with many antique houses, and with altogether a rural and picturesque aspect, unlike anything in America, and yet processing a familiar look, as if it were something I had dreamed about.'

**Nathaniel Hawthorne, 1854**

'Along the shore is a narrow, unsafe promenade, called Aquarium Parade, but perhaps better known as 'Ham & Egg Terrace' the favourite resort of the Liverpool and Lancashire trippers and roughs...Here are stationed the eating house and refreshment room keepers, whose constant solicitations to dine early and often are such a nuisance.'

**Phillip Sulley, The Hundred of Wirral, 1889**

'For here is Port Sunlight, its blocks of trim houses showing many interesting styles of architecture, with lawns and nice little gardens in front of each house, and, in many cases, ivy or climbing plants clinging to the walls.'

**Harold Young, Perambulation of the Hundred of Wirral, 1909**

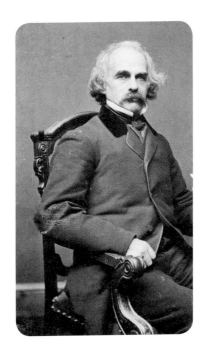

# Famous For...

### The Mersey Ferry

The famous Mersey ferries actually originate from Birkenhead and not Liverpool as it is often assumed. Benedictine monks based at Birkenhead Priory offered safe passage across the river to travellers wishing to attend the markets that once took place in Liverpool over the water. Back then the city was only a small fishing village, but nowadays thousands of visitors climb aboard the ferries each year in order to take in the unique views of the Merseyside waterfronts.

### Variety

Wirral is a place of true variety, with densely populated urban conurbations sitting within minutes of tree-filled countryside and open farmland. From the terraced houses of Rock Ferry to the grand houses in leafy Oxton village, Wirral is a genuine melting pot of people and social diversity. The more affluent areas of Hoylake and Heswall have the largest number of residents aged over 75, whilst Bidston, Seacombe and Tranmere, traditional dockland areas, are currently home to the greatest proportion of children.

Wirral accents also differ widely. Those nearest the river Mersey can be expected to speak in a more recognised 'Scouse' accent, whilst those from the south of the borough may well have a more Cheshire-like intonation.

## Industrial Heritage

Wirral has a strong industrial heritage with a number of the most successful businesses originating in the Victorian era. In 1824 William Laird established a boiler works on Wallasey Pool. With the assistance of his son John, the company diversified to become one of the world's chief shipbuilding enterprises. Birkenhead's first docks opened in 1847 to much acclaim and contributed to the area's future success and maritime prosperity. In ceramics, Harold Steward Rathbone and Conrad Dressler were responsible for founding the Della Robbia studio. Although they were never particularly successful in their time, pieces of Della Robbia are now highly sought after the world over. In 1887 William Lever founded the village Port Sunlight to expand his successful soap-making company Sunlight Soap. By the 1930s the firm was making 4,000 tons of soap a week.

## Holidays

At one time New Brighton was a real haven for holidaymakers. With its 3.5km promenade the resort has featured many popular attractions over the years, such as the world's largest open-air swimming pool, a model boating lake, a funfair complete with circus and a soaring tower and ballroom which had been the tallest building in Britain on opening in 1900. With the rise in affordable foreign holidays during the twentieth century, UK holiday resorts such as New Brighton fell into decline, but more recently there has been noticeable resurgence with the town set to become a popular leisure destination once again.

## The Birthplace of Englishness

In 2004 a team of academics believed they had found the battlefield where the concept of 'Englishness' was born. The Battle at Brunanburh in AD 937 was fought by King Athelstan when he united the Anglo-Saxons for the first time to repel a Viking invasion, changing the course of history forever. Their research claimed that the site of the battle mentioned in the Anglo-Saxon Chronicle was on what is now a golf course on Brackenwood Road, Bebington.

## Birkenhead Park

The world's first publicly funded park is actually Birkenhead Park, which was opened in 1847 to the designs of the respected architect Joseph Paxton. 125 acres of land were designated for public use, with another 60 acres offered for private residential development. The proceeds from the sales of building plots were sufficient to recoup all the costs incurred and the project was hailed a great commercial and social success. So inspiring was the creation that American landscape architect Frederick Law Olmsted used many of the features in his design for New York's now world-renowned Central Park after he visited Wirral in 1850. Birkenhead Park was designated a conservation area in 1977 and declared a Grade I listed landscape in 1995. It remains one of Wirral's most popular beauty spots.

# Infamous For...

## Social and Economic Decline

Throughout the latter part of the twentieth century Merseyside fell into a steep decline resulting in a fall in living conditions and job prospects. The terrible deprivation of the period contributed to the 1981 Toxteth riots in Liverpool. This was the point when the whole county began to finally take notice. Government minister Michael Heseltine was sent to Merseyside to set up initiatives and improve conditions for the local population, thirty years on Merseyside's reputation has greatly improved.

## Public Pyjamas

In a number of places across the country it is not uncommon to catch sight of a certain few people in the neighbourhood dressed only in their pyjamas. Parts of Wirral have also fallen foul to this practice. This cringe-worthy fashion trend has been the catalyst of some heated debate between social commentators which has even spread abroad. Opinions are split over the contentious issue with Dr Helen Churchill of Liverpool John Moores University remarking, 'The interesting question isn't why people wear pyjamas, but why other people think it's a problem to do so. After all, they can be warm and practical. We should celebrate the wearing of pyjamas in public.' Many others, however, view the garments to be plain lazy and even unhygienic for everyday use.

## Misidentification

More often than not, Wirral is hidden from the world stage by the overbearing shadow of our big sister Liverpool. Wirral's inhabitants are often clumped together as Liverpudlians but people on both sides of the Mersey hold this social amalgamation with quiet disdain. The not so endearing term 'Plazzy Scouser' is a description of Wirralians bestowed on us by our cross-river friends. It alludes to our pseudo-Scouse status, especially people residing in towns dotted along the edge of Mersey where the city's social influence is strongest and most apparent.

# Wirral in Days Gone By:
# Landing Stage, Woodside

# Making the Headlines

### 29 July 1929

The third World Scout Jamboree was held at Arrowe Park
and also commemorated the 21st birthday of Scouting.
Over 50,000 Scouts and Girl Guides from across the world
attended, including the founder of the movement, General
Baden-Powell. Vast interest was aroused merely by the
nature of such a rally with 320,000 visitors often braving bad
weather to witness the event. They were treated to superb
Scout displays and wonderful pageants, demonstrations and
sing-alongs never before seen in England.

### 18 July 1934

Over 200,000 people gathered to watch King George V
and Queen Mary officially open the Queensway Tunnel.
The link provided a roadway under the river Mersey, directly
connecting Liverpool to Wirral. It was a truly epic engineering
accomplishment taking nearly a decade to construct. At over
2 miles long, it was the largest sub-aqueous tunnel ever built
and the marvel of a whole generation.

### 18 November 1983

Janet Walton hit the headlines by giving birth to the world's
only known set of all-female sextuplets. The Waltons had
almost given up on having children when their thirteenth
attempt at fertility treatment gave rise to spectacular results.
The Liverpool couple moved to Wallasey to bring up their
huge brood in an eight-bedroom house. Hannah, Luci, Ruth,
Sarah, Kate and Jennifer still live on Wirral today and try to
get together every weekend for a very large Sunday roast at
the family home.

49

## 7 March 2011

Protesters made the press when hundreds of campaigners stormed Birkenhead County Court to make a citizens' arrest on Judge Michael Peake. Their actions were in support of the anti-establishment British Constitution Group (BCG) who were championing local resident Roger Hayes for challenging his council tax bill. Raymond Saintclair, who organised the protest, said, 'Today was day one. This is going to happen again and again and again. We have sent a message to this court as one nation and one voice until change comes.' Mr Hayes, however, was later committed to prison for twenty-one days for arrears and costs of £1,477.14 and his wilful refusal to pay.

## 1 June 2012

The Olympic torch made its way through Wirral on its way to the London Summer Olympics. Former Spice Girl Mel C and the borough's Olympic Gold cyclist Chris Boardman carried the torch along with several deserving locals. Runners included Alice Cavanagh, Becki Blacklock and Ben Osu, who had all made a difference to the local community. It was estimated that around 60,000 people lined the relay's route with 25,000 filling Birkenhead Park for a colossal festival of sports and fitness.

# Letters to the Press

### 18 August 1860

'I was much pleased to observe a few days ago that Mr Train has at length induced the authorities of Birmingham, Manchester and Glasgow to grant him permission to lay down tramways in those important cities. The new and improved method of street locomotion, there can be little doubt, will prove beneficial as the comparison between the omnibus and horse railway is so great that upon the introduction of the latter, the former clumsy vehicle will be almost altogether discarded by the public so that in the course of a very short time, we may expect to see the street railway universally and permanently adopted in all our principal towns and cities. In a few days we shall have the pleasure of witnessing the American system in full and active operation at Birkenhead when everyone who has any doubt upon the matter will be able to decide for himself which of the two is the most pleasant and most agreeable mode of travelling.'

Go-Ahead

### 28 May 1887

'Last summer I visited the lending department of the free library, sometimes during the evenings, and I felt sorry to find the assistants employed in that department were working (with the exception of Saturday) up to nine o'clock every evening. Could not the committee see its way to closing the lending department at six or seven o'clock in the summer months, to enable the assistants to get a little fresh air, cricket or other recreation? I feel sure that everyone would be glad to get or change their books before that hour. The reading room should certainly remain open til the usual hour as that could easily be managed by a smaller staff.'

M.L.P.

### 19 December 1918

'Just now the public are anxiously looking forward to a reduction in prices; instead we find the Wallasey Tramway Company are increasing the car fares by 50 per cent, charging a penny less than a mile and giving, I should say, the poorest value for money in the country. Everyone one meets is disgusted about it.'

J.L.

### 3 March 2009

'Oh dear, I am so sorry I offended the reader who berated me for daring to state that Wirral is a Cheshire peninsula (which it is) and told me to come off my high horse, which I did at the local riding school. Far from being in "another century" the reader concerned appears to have forgotten that Merseyside was created in 1974, along with Greater Manchester, Humberside, Tayside, *et al*. None of these are proper counties, they are artificial and political.
The traditional counties are part of the UK and have been around for centuries, historically and geographically, and must be kept.'

Miss P. Lord, Thingwall.

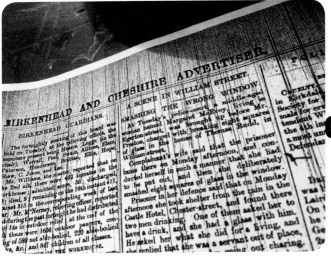

## BIRKENHEAD AND CHESHIRE ADVERTISER.

### BIRKENHEAD GUARDIANS.

The fortnightly meeting of this board was held on Tuesday at the relieving office, the members present being Messrs. Legge (in the chair), Worrall, Poole, Swain, Allison, Elain, Paterson, Henderson, and Lee.

Mr. Williams, the master, reported that on the 2nd ult. there were 403 inmates in the workhouse; admitted since, 56; discharged, ...; died, 8 ... remaining on the 16th instant 411 ... in the corresponding week of last ...

Mr. M'Nerney, relieving officer, reported that during the past fortnight he had distributed ... 14s in out-door relief at the end of the ... these were 1656 outdoor paupers, con-... of 589 not able-bodied, 220 able-bodied ..., &c., and 847 children of all classes.

... THE WORKHOUSE.

### A SCENE IN WILLIAM STREET.

#### SMASHING THE WRONG WINDOW.

At Tuesday's police court a middle-aged woman named Margaret M'Avoy, living in Egerton-street, was brought up before Mr. Preston, charged with breaking eight square of glass in the house of Thomas Rudd, in William-street.

Complainant's wife said that the prisoner came there on Monday afternoon, and conducted herself in such a manner that she had to be put out, and then she deliberately smashed eight squares of glass in the window.

Prisoner in her defence said that on Monday afternoon she took shelter from the rain in the Castle Hotel, Chester-street, and found there two men drinking. One of them asked her to have a drink, and she had a glass with him. He asked her what she did for a living, and she replied that she was a servant out of place, ... going out charing.

### POLI...

CRUELTY ...
was ... in Kirkdal... Society for ... mals for cr... tendent W... the 4th in... a most un... Defendan...

Da...
was ...
Lair...
On ...
he ...
Ge...
2...

# Rebellious Wirral

In 1879 numerous strikes swept across the region with dock labourers and merchant seaman demanding better pay. By February, 150 Birkenhead porters employed at the grain warehouses at the Great Float joined in the general movement. Just after seven o'clock on the morning of the 11th, 1,000 inactive men assembled at the docks to await the arrival of those heading to work. There were reports of angry jeering and hollering which resulted in a departure from work by those who had otherwise intended to earn a living that day. The foremen and deliverymen, however, stuck to their posts but several large steamers were left with the majority of their cargoes unprocessed. By this point 25,000 workers stood idle, bringing the Merseyside maritime trade to its knees.

In 1919 Wirral was swept up in a police strike which crippled many forces across the country. It was in that year that the National Union of Police and Prison Officers called a strike after the government voted through measures to prevent them ever doing so. A policeman's job was very difficult and while a labourer could expect a wage of about £3 7s a week, a constable's could be as low as £2 3s with far longer hours. There was a general consensus amongst officers that a powerful statement had to be made. Up to 10 per cent of police in London and Birmingham refused to patrol, but it was the coppers of Merseyside who made the biggest impact. More than half the Liverpool and Birkenhead forces, as well as three quarters of the police in nearby Bootle, hung up their handcuffs and left their boots unpolished. It was also the people of Merseyside who were the most seriously affected by the consequences of the action, when public disorder and looting became all too common. Several weeks into the rebellion virtually all the striking Bobbies had been permanently replaced by men from outside the region and public support for the cause was beginning to die down. Despite the apparent failure of the strike, police staff later received pay increases and successive governments began to take real notice of an officer's working conditions.

In more recent years Wirral students took to the Town Hall in Wallasey to protest against a rise in university tuition fees. Over 100 prospective academics from schools and colleges across the peninsula armed themselves with placards to air their common sentiment in November 2010. Backed by the National Union of Students, this event was one of many protests across the country in an effort to persuade the government to cancel plans which allowed universities to charge up to £9,000 a year in fees. Many more took to the streets of Liverpool to join 2,000 others in marches and sit down protests throughout the city centre. Their plight was unsuccessful and now learners across the UK will incur thousands of pounds of debt before even finishing their course.

# Buildings: the Best

## Hamilton Square

The magnificent Hamilton Square has been described as the jewel in Wirral's crown since its celebrated foundation. Built in 1826 by leading Edinburgh architect James Gillespie Graham, it was the brainchild and dream of entrepreneur William Laird, whose vision was to build a new and respectable town near to his flourishing shipyard. Hamilton Square was to be the centre and lined with elegant houses and luscious private gardens for the enjoyment of the well-to-do of Wirral society. Space was left on a prime spot for the addition of a noble town hall on which work began in 1883. Birkenhead Town Hall was finally opened four years later by Laird's young daughter Elsie to a gathering of 5,000 spectators. Built with Scottish granite, local Storeton sandstone and topped with Welsh slate to the design of Charles Ellison, this stunning structure was completed by an iconic 200ft clock tower. It continues to be one of the country's grandest public squares today with many of the old mansion houses converted to sought-after apartments and business locations.

## Lady Lever Art Gallery

After Lady Lever's death from pneumonia in 1913, a devastated Lord Lever set about making plans to honour her memory. The following year, designs for a brand new art gallery had been finalised and its construction was soon underway. In March 1914, the foundation stone for the Lady Lever Art Gallery was laid down by King George V and Queen Mary via a remote control from Hulme Hall. It was built with Portland Stone clad over a body of reinforced concrete. Marble bases were included at each of the entrance steps with doors on the south of the building flanked with stone urns. In 1930 a remarkable memorial obelisk was erected in honour of Lord Lever who had by then passed away himself. This was designed by his godson, James Lomax Simpson, and sculptured impeccably from bronze and granite. The figures at its base represent Industry, Education, Charity and Art. Inspiration stands high on top. It was these traits that were thought to most successfully represent Lord Lever's long and tireless work for Port Sunlight.

## New Brighton Perch Rock

One of the more unusual features on Wirral's landscape has to be New Brighton's Fort, which was built in 1829 at a cost of just under £27,000. Fear of a Napoleonic attack on shipping interests in the city of Liverpool forced officials to make plans to protect the strategic seaport. Sixteen large mounted guns were installed about the defensive battery, along with enough accommodation to house 100 military personnel. In 1939, fifteen minutes after the announcement of war, Fort Commander Cocks gave the order for two shots to be fired at a mysterious vessel seen entering the closed waters. The boat turned out to be an innocent fisherman, but these may well have been the first ever shots of the Second World War. The structure was eventually demobilised in the 1950s and sold at auction to private owners. It has changed hands several times but is now owned by the Darroch family who have opened it to the public with a number of displays and exhibitions on show.

## Hadlow Road Station

Well worth a visit is Hadlow Road in the village of Willaston. It features a very quaint railway station on the old Hooton to West Kirby line of the Birkenhead Railway. It was opened back in 1866 to serve the small population of Willaston which then stood at far less than 1,000. The station closed to passengers in 1956 but the track continued to be used for freight transportation and driver training for another six years. In the 1970s the route became part of the Wirral Way footpath and part of Wirral Country Park. In doing so it was the first such designated site in Britain. Nostalgically the majority of the station has been preserved to give an authentic 1950s look and a short section of track has even been re-laid in front of the eastbound platform. Hadlow Road Station is now a very popular and eye-pleasing Grade II listed treasure and one of the best attractions Wirral has to offer.

# Buildings: the Worst

### Asda, Birkenhead

In 2011 work was completed on a brand new Asda store in Birkenhead representing a much needed £30 million investment to the town centre. However this 90,000 square foot monster fronts onto Grange Road, Exmouth Street, Claughton Road, Catherine Street and Saint John Street! It's safe to say this is the largest building the town centre has ever seen and it certainly cannot be missed. Unfortunately the architecture is far from spectacular with prison-like grey walls and bland beige supporting segments. Supermarkets aren't generally known for their aesthetic appeal and in this respect, Asda does not disappoint.

### The Concourse, West Kirby

Sitting close to West Kirby railway station is a somewhat intimidating construction known as the Concourse. This is without a doubt a very useful building, housing the local library, a medical centre, a sports centre complete with 25m swimming pool, as well as a One Stop Shop. Nevertheless, its valuable and community-spirited purpose does not help make this 1970s building look less than awful and has been subject to much local debate. In 2005 Jeff Clarke, a Liberal Democrat Parliamentary Spokesman for Wirral West, raised concerns about the area and its apparent deprivation. He branded the lack of investment in the tired-looking Concourse 'unacceptable' and remarked, 'West Kirby residents deserve better.' To date there has been little progress, much to the frustration of many in the area.

### Civic Way, Bebington

Civic Way was built mid-twentieth century over land once occupied by Bebington Old Hall. Sadly the beautiful Georgian property was demolished to make way for several new buildings including a town hall, council offices, a library and a police station. With hindsight it is clear that this unimaginative complex is a colourless mistake offering nothing to the aesthetic of this otherwise pleasing neighbourhood.

# Historic Miscellany

The diary of Henry Totty, a Heswall farmer, records numerous events in the development of the town in the nineteenth century. His notes include the construction of a 'large house on the hill' in March 1870. This was Heswall Castle, soon nicknamed Titherington's Folly due to the owner's wife, Mrs Titherington, taking an immediate dislike to the place and refusing to live there. It later became an orphanage.

The naming of the Wirral suburb of Spital has interesting origins. The label was often given to a place or building which acted as a hospital or colony for lepers. However, it may have also derived its name from the word 'hospitality' due to the large proportion of people who worked as servants on the nearby Poulton estate.

The Tranmere Cross dates back to the 1400s when it probably stood in Church Road. It vanished in the 1860s but was discovered seventy years later being used as a sundial at the entrance to Tranmere New Hall. It was reinstated in Victoria Park in 1935.

Emma Hamilton, the well-known mistress of Lord Horatio Nelson, is believed to have been born in the village of Ness under the name Amy Lyons. She was the daughter of a humble blacksmith who died when she was a child. Amy was brought up in Hawarden, North Wales by her mother but went on to become something of a popular socialite in high-ranking London society. She met Nelson in 1798 and from then on one of world's most famous love affairs began to blossom. Sadly ten years after Nelson's heroic death at the Battle of Trafalgar, Emma died penniless in 1815. The British Government had largely ignored Nelson's wishes to provide for her and their daughter Horatia, leaving Emma to fall into a life of debt-ridden poverty in Calais.

The Wheatsheaf Inn can be found in the sleepy hamlet of Raby and is thought to have been a public house since 1611. Further research has discovered that a farm licensed to brew and sell beer since the thirteenth century once existed here. This makes Raby one of the oldest hostelries in the country.

In 1939 Chapman's Travelling Zoo and Circus were performing in the car park of Tranmere Rovers football ground. After a performance two tigers, Romeo and Bengal, were being led back to their cages when they made a break for it. One fled to the big top and was quickly recaptured. The other leapt into the gardens of houses in Borough Road but was coaxed into the garage of No.745. After a brief nap he was soon persuaded back into his cage without any further upset.

# Museums and Galleries

Birkenhead Priory

Fort Perch Rock

Lady Lever Art Gallery

Port Sunlight Museum

Spaceport

The U-Boat Story

The Wilfred Owen Story and Gallery

Williamson Art Gallery

Wirral Transport Museum

West Kirby Museum

# Parks and Green Spaces

Arrowe Country Park

Ashton Park

Bidston Hill

Birkenhead Park

Caldy Hill

Central Park

Dibbinsdale Nature Reserve

Eastham Country Park

Heswall Dales

Hilbre Island

Mersey Park

Ness Botanic Gardens

North Wirral Coastal Park

Royden Park

Stapledon Woods

Thursaston Common

Vale Park

Victoria Park

Wirral Country Park

# Businesses

## Cammell Laird

Birkenhead grew to considerable size and importance
thanks to the Laird shipyard. Founded by William Laird,
a Scottish businessman, the company quickly became pre-
eminent in nautical manufacture. In 1903 Laird joined forces
with the Sheffield-based metallurgists Johnson Cammell
& Co. to create Cammell Laird, the name which exists today.
The yard is notable for producing the *Ma Robert*, built in
1858 for Dr Livingstone's Zambezi expedition, the 1862
CSS *Alabama* built for the Confederate States of America and
HMS *Caroline* in 1914 which holds the record for the fastest
build time of any significant warship (nine months from her
keel being laid till her launch). They also constructed the
first all-welded ship, the *Fullagar*, in 1920, the aircraft carrier
HMS *Ark Royal* in 1938 and a later carrier of the same name
and the most powerful in the navy, in 1955. The firm is still
in operation today, focussing on ship repair and employing
approximately 700 members of staff.

## Lee's Tapestry Works

Arthur Lee set up his first tapestry works in Warrington in
1888, but moved the growing operation to busy Birkenhead
twenty years later. At its peak the firm employed over 400
people who all played their part in making the firm globally
famous for spectacular quality materials and tapestries.
Their work was found in palaces, chanceries, boardrooms,
embassies and even inside the Royal carriages of trains. One of
the most famous customers of the works was Jacqueline
Kennedy, wife of President John Kennedy. Economic pressures
and mass-produced competition forced the closure of the
company in 1970, but the management successfully found
new positions for every member of staff elsewhere.

75

## Burtons Foods

George Burton began producing biscuits in Blackpool in the mid-1800s. Under the family's stewardship, Burton's bakery became a leading supplier of snacks to UK households. However in 2011 its Wirral-based chocolate refinery was forced to make savings with the loss of over 200 jobs. The makers of well-loved products such as Jammie Dodgers, Wagon Wheels and Maryland cookies said it planned to invest more into its Edinburgh and Llantarnam sites, but would keep a small percentage of its Wirral workers. A representative of Burton's Foods said it was a 'regrettable' decision at a time when, although the company was growing in sales, it faced 'significant cost pressures'. Wallasey MP Angela Eagle stated, 'While I welcome the decision to retain the chocolate refinery, which will leave around forty-five jobs on site, it is heart-breaking that the sixty-year tradition of biscuit making in Moreton will now come to an end.'

## Lever Brothers

Despondent with the lack of opportunities in the grocery world, brothers William and James Lever entered the soap business in 1885. They brought a small soap works in Warrington and soon teamed up with William Hough Watson. He had invented a novel process which created a soap comprised of glycerin and vegetable oils. This later became known as Sunlight Soap and within three years production had reached a whopping 450 tons per week. Larger premises were built on marshes at Bromborough Pool which became Port Sunlight. In 1930, it merged with the Dutch business Margarine Unie, to form Unilever, the first recognised multinational company in modern times. The company makes a wide range of products from Persil to Lynx and continues to use its original Port Sunlight factory in its global operations.

# Political Figures

### Frederick Smith

Born in Birkenhead in 1872, Frederick Smith was a Conservative statesman and lawyer. He was a skilled orator, noted for his staunch opposition to Irish nationalism and pugnacious views. After studying at several schools in the North West he went to Oxford where he became the President of the Oxford Union. Later he became one of the highest paid barristers in the country, making over £10,000 per annum. His most famous success was the defence of Ethel le Neve, the mistress of the infamous Dr Crippen. In 1906 he became MP for Walton before achieving the position of Attorney General and at age 47, Lord Chancellor. He was a close friend of Winston Churchill despite the two often holding very different points of view. Smith died in London in 1930 with the title First Earl of Birkenhead.

### Glenda Jackson

The double Oscar-winning actress turned politician Glenda Jackson was born in Birkenhead in 1936. The daughter of a bricklayer, Glenda successfully gained a place at West Kirkby Grammar School for girls, later studying drama at RADA. After a very successful career on stage and screen, Jackson retired from acting in order to enter the House of Commons in the 1992 general election as the Labour MP for Hampstead and Highgate. In May 2010 boundary changes saw Jackson elected as the MP for the new Hampstead and Kilburn constituency, which she won by a tiny margin. The following year, Jackson announced that she would not seek re-election at the next vote: 'I will be almost 80 and by then it will be time for someone else to have a turn.'

## Harold Wilson

Former Prime Minister Harold Wilson has strong links to Wirral. He was a wartime baby born in Huddersfield 1916, but aged 14 his father moved the family to Bromborough to find employment as an industrial chemist. The ambitious teenager enrolled at Wirral Grammar School where he became their first Head Boy. He went on to study Philosophy, Politics and Economics at Oxford and later became the Labour MP for Ormskirk, and then Huyton, when boundary changes came into effect. Wilson was Prime Minister for two terms during his lifetime and resigned in 1976 aged 60. His achievements included proposing the idea of the Open University, improving road safety regulations, keeping Britain out of the Vietnam War, and championing new technology. In 2013 it was reported that a memorial stone will be installed in West Minister Abbey in honour of Wilson who passed away in 1995.

## Frank Field

Frank Field has been the MP for Birkenhead since 1979 and is seen as a strong political veteran by all parties. Originally from London, Field studied Economics at the University of Hull before entering the teaching profession. His interest in politics led him to become a councillor for the borough of Hounslow and later the director of the Child Poverty Action Group and the Low Pay Unit. Since winning the safe seat of Birkenhead, Field has successfully retained his position and actually raised his majority at the last election. In 2010 he was given the role of 'Poverty Czar' in David Cameron's coalition government, advising the cabinet on how best to tackle problems in the country's most deprived areas. In doing so he is the first member of the Labour Party to have a role within Cameron's team.

Sapientia
Ianua
Vitae

Sapientia
Ianua
Vitae

SAPIENTIA IANUAVITAE

# Wirral Firsts

The world's first publically-funded park is Birkenhead Park, completed in 1847. Its surroundings are built on former swampland which took approximately 1,000 men four years to convert to usable acreage. It was the inspiration for New York's Central Park.

Europe's first street tramway opened in Wirral on 30 August 1860. The first line ran from Woodside transporting passengers through town along Argyle Street, down Conway Street and to the grand entrance of Birkenhead Park. This early system was horse-drawn and was the brainchild of flamboyant American, George Francis Train. Each car could accommodate up to sixty commuters.

In 1896, Birkenhead's Argyle Theatre was the first outside of London to present Thomas Edison's Living Pictures. In 1910 it showed footage from the funeral of King Edward VII and in 1911, the coronation of King George and Queen Mary. The Argyle was also the first music hall to air radio broadcasts throughout the Commonwealth and the only British music hall to broadcast direct to the United States via a coast-to-coast hook-up.

The world's first Boy Scout Troop was formed in Wirral in 1908. That year Baden-Powell publically inaugurated the movement in a speech at the YMCA in Birkenhead's Grange Road. The first and second Scout Huts were established in the town and the latter is still in existence today at the corner of Borough Road and North Road.

The first commercial shore-based radar station in the world for the navigation of ships was installed at Seacombe ferry terminal in 1947.

The world's first passenger hovercraft service operated between Moreton and Rhyl, North Wales on 20 July 1962. It became known as a Hover Coach but strong winds and rough seas made the service unviable after only nineteen days in service.

## BIRKENHEAD MUNICIPAL TRANSPORT

# HOVERCRAFT SERVICE
### (Operated by B.U.A. Ltd.)

# MORETON TO RHYL
## COMMENCING FRIDAY, 20th JULY

DON'T FAIL TO SEE THE WORLD'S FIRST HOVERCRAFT IN PUBLIC SERVICE.

HOVERCRAFT LEAVES MORETON SHORE DAILY EXCEPT TUESDAYS AT INTERVALS BETWEEN 10.15 A.M. AND 6.45 P.M.

CORPORATION BUSES, ROUTES Nos. 22, 77 AND 87 WILL TAKE YOU DIRECT TO THE STARTING POINT AT MORETON SHORE.

---

G. A. CHERRY,
General Manager.

TRANSPORT OFFICES,
LAIRD STREET.
JULY, 1962.

# Crime and the Macabre

At a County Court sitting on 10 August 1869, Frederick Welmin sued his former employer Edward Logan for alleged overdue wages. Welmin had been Logan's butler at Thurstaston Hall, but he was unceremoniously sacked due to drunkenness on duty. The offence had taken place during a dinner party at which Welmin was unable to distinguish one dish from another, causing the utmost embarrassment to the host. He even spoke to guests as if he was one himself, amusing some but annoying others. On his discharge Welmin accepted £3 16s but was now seeking more. Judge Harden thought the plaintiff was pushing his luck and threw the case out.

By the late 1880s the fortunes of Isambard Kingdom Brunel's gigantic vessel SS *Great Eastern* had well and truly faded. It had been the largest ship ever built, but by then her only use was as a huge floating advertisement board for Lewis Department store. The decision was finally made to send her for scrap in 1889 on the sands at Rock Ferry. During the dismantlement a mysterious skeleton was discovered in an inner compartment; one which had not been explored for decades. The remains may well have been all that was left of one unfortunate labourer who had worked on the original fitting of the ship some forty years earlier.

On 9 September 1900, post office clerk George Fell was brutally murdered by an unknown killer. When fellow employees had finished their Sunday morning shift, the fifty-six year old was left alone at the office in Conway Street, Birkenhead. At some point Fell answered the door to the sorting room in Burlington Street where he was immediately assaulted. His blood was found in the hallway, up the stairs and in the telegraph office where he had obviously fled in absolute terror. His attempts to defend himself with a coal shovel proved useless and the man's skull was caved in by a fireplace poker. The killer placed a sorting bag over the dead man's face before making off with £142 17s 8d from the safe. His disguise was the victim's own post office coat. Attempts to locate the money through serial numbers were unsuccessful and the murderer was never found.

In 1905 Ralph Aspinall was charged 20$s$ or face one month's imprisonment. Police Constable Morris had caught him red-handed, stealing roses from the garden of James McNaughten in Acres Road, Bebington.

Fourteen-year-old Edith Eaton was the unfortunate victim of an attempted murder in 1907. She had been alone in the house, lying in bed, when twenty-two-year-old Ernest Cliffe crept into the property at No. 82 Beaconsfield Road, New Ferry. He attempted to cut her throat with a razor blade but her will to survive was too great. Her cries attracted the attention of her next-door neighbour whose presence brought a halt to the dreadful proceedings. After failing to drown himself, Cliffe was arrested and charged with the attack. His defence, that the young Edith had been mocking him for weeks and he was sick of it, was categorically denied by her. The prisoner was sentenced to five years in custody.

On 10 January 1925, the body of eleven-year-old Nellie Clarke was found slumped against a telegraph pole behind Spenser Avenue in Rock Ferry. She had been sent out on an errand at around 8.10 p.m. but failed to return home to Byrne Avenue. An investigation revealed she had been raped and strangled, but her callous killer was never discovered.

NELLIE CLARKE
THE VICTIM OF THE
FOUL MURDER
PORTRAIT TAKEN FROM
A SCHOOL GROUP.

THE BLOODHOUND WHICH WAS
ASSISTING IN THE SEARCH FOR
THE MURDERER. SERGT. ASTBURY IS
SHOWN CARRYING A BOX CONTAINING
A STOCKING OF THE MURDERED GIRL.

HIGHFIELD ROAD

X O  SHORT
       PASSAGE

LONG
ENTRY

SPENCER AVENUE

SKETCH SHOWING THE
SPOT WHERE THE BODY
WAS FOUND . PROPPED
AGAINST A TELEGRAPH
POST IN THE SHORT
PASSAGE LEADING
FROM SPENCER AVENUE

# Ghosts

At Port Sunlight's Bridge Inn customers may see more than the spirits in their glasses. Marie McNally and David Thomas took over as licensees of the pub in 2008, where the figures of a soldier, a merchant seaman, a young servant girl and a distinguished gentleman smoking a cigar have all been reported. One guest also reported that her bed was shaken by a mysterious force during her one-night stay at the premises.

There have been several sightings of monks in the grounds of St Andrews in Bebington. A church has been on this site since before the Norman Conquest and the Domesday Book records a priest in Bebington as early as 1086. Many people have spoken of seeing ghostly apparitions of monks leaving the churchyard and walking towards the old collegiate house in nearby Kirket Lane.

Thursaston Hall is said to be home to the ghost of a deeply agitated woman. The figure has been seen in the west wing bedrooms and appears to be very distraught, wringing her hands, and looking for something. She was last seen in 1980, when a team of archaeologists from Liverpool University witnessed the phantom peering out from a window.

In 1937, there were a number of reports regarding a startling apparition that had been seen near Victoria Park. An elderly couple returning from an evening visit to a friend in Devonshire Park had run into a police station in a very frantic state telling the bemused desk sergeant that they had seen a ghastly glowing face. Moments later, a constable raced in stuttering out his own description of the glowing head. He had just seen it floating up Church Road by St Catherine's Hospital.

# Wirral at War

The first fatality of the Merseyside Blitz occurred in Wirral when bombs rained down on the night of 9 August 1940. They claimed the life of Johanna Mandale, a servant of the Bunney family in Prenton Lane.

Wirral and Merseyside would go on to suffer extensive damage throughout the remainder of the Second World War. Merseyside was the most bombed location outside of London due to the important shipping industries based on its shorelines. The May Blitz of 1941 was particularly destructive. There was an intense loss of life and injuries were in abundance. In total the Nazis brought death to approximately 4,000 of Merseyside's inhabitants and left her remaining residents with mental scars and atrocious blemishes on their local landscape.

# Notable Residents

### William Ralph Dean

Dixie Dean, as he was known, was born in Birkenhead in 1907. After displaying his skills with a number of amateur local teams, including Laird Street School, Moreton Bible Class and Heswall and Pensby United, the young prodigy signed up to Tranmere Rovers in 1923. The club was struggling at the bottom of the Third Division but Dean secured twenty-seven goals in thirty games. Two years later he joined Everton with a considerable transfer fee of £3,000, becoming their top scorer for the club that season. Dean went on to become the most prolific goal-scorer in English football history and his famous exploits during the 1927–28 season saw him score sixty league goals. A statue of Dean was unveiled outside Goodison Park in May 2001 and the following year he became one of twenty-two players inducted into the inaugural English Football Hall of Fame. He passed away watching a game at his beloved Goodison in 1980. His funeral took place at St James Church, Birkenhead.

### Wilfred Owen

One of the world's most illustrious war poets, Wilfred Owen was famous for poems such as, 'Anthem for Doomed Youth', 'Futility' and 'Dulce et Decorum est'. Born in Oswestry, the death of his grandfather in 1897 saw the family lose their home and move to more modest means in Birkenhead. The Owens lived in several properties in the area, including Elm Road, Wilmer Road and Milton Road. In 1915 Owen enlisted in the army and was commissioned into the Manchester Regiment, heading to the Western Front early in January 1917. After experiencing heavy fighting, he was diagnosed with shellshock and sent back home to recover. 1918 saw Owen returned to active service in France where he was killed in action exactly one week before the signing of the Armistice. His shocking and realistic war poetry revealed the true terror of the conflict and continues to serve as a lasting reminder to future generations.

DIXIE DEAN
EVERTON F. CLUB

## Charles Joughin

Charles Joughin was born in Birkenhead's Patten Street in the year 1879. He progressed through his trade as a baker and served on a number of liners including the ill-fated White Star vessel, RMS *Titanic*. He was one of the fortunate few to survive the disaster despite being in the water for over two hours; a feat many at the time put down to his downing of half a tumbler of liquor before the sinking. At an official inquiry, Charles described how he had actually ridden the ship down into the icy waters of the Atlantic and treaded water until being rescued. 'My head may have been wetted, but no more,' he said in his testimony. It was this amazing act which went on to inspire similar final scenes in James Cameron's 1997 eponymous blockbuster.

## Andrew Irvine

The intrepid Andrew 'Sandy' Irvine was born in Birkenhead in 1902. Aged only 22 he took part in the 1924 British Everest Expedition, the third British expedition to the world's highest mountain. Whilst attempting the first ascent, he and his climbing partner George Mallory, who was only one year his senior, vanished somewhere on the mountain's north-east ridge. The pair were last sighted only a few hundred metres from the summit. Mallory's frozen body was discovered in 1999 and the find rekindled decades-old debates about whether he and Irvine had finally reached the top. If so, the pair would have beaten Sir Edmund Hillary's historic feat by several decades. Irvine's body is still lost on the mountain eighty-nine years after he began the ascent.

## Albert Laver

On 18 December 2012, a special memorial was unveiled in honour of one of Wirral's most heroic sons. Royal Marine Albert Laver was one of the 'Cockleshell Heroes' whose brave raid on Nazi vessels in 1942 was credited with shortening the war by six months. Laver and nine other young men completed 70 miles of upriver paddling in canoes to Bordeaux. They succeeded in sinking one ship, severely damaging four others and inflicting enough impairment to the port that its use was greatly disrupted for months. Wirral mayor Gerry Ellis and former Liberal Democrat leader Paddy Ashdown officially unveiled the important plaque on the promenade at Woodside.

# Celebrity Connections

Wirral has a number of celebrity connections. Here is a small selection:

## Paul O'Grady

Paul O'Grady made it famous with his comedic portrayal of the blond bombshell Lily Savage. He was born at St Catherine's Hospital and spent his early life at the family home in Holly Grove, Tranmere, attending St Joseph's Primary School as an infant. After working at various locations across Merseyside, including the RAFA club in Oxton and a Children's Convalescent Home in West Kirby, he left Wirral and headed to London to continue his work in social care. It was a whole new experience for Paul. 'As a kid, Birkenhead was my world, there was nowhere outside it,' he said in a 2008 interview. Paul made a name for himself on the capital's comedy circuit and national stardom followed throughout the 1980s and beyond. He has since enjoyed a successful career distinct from his drag queen creation and is now a much-loved radio and television personality known for his down-to-earth and candid persona.

## Eric Idle

*Monty Python* star Eric Idle may have been born in South Shields, but he has fond memories of living in Wirral as a child. In an interview with the *Liverpool Daily Post* in 2010, he recalled his time in Wallasey where he had been a pupil at St George's Primary School. 'It was lovely, I love Wallasey.' He was sent off to a boarding school in Wolverhampton at the age of 7 where he remained until adulthood. 'Wallasey had been a lovely place to be and there I was stuck in Wolverhampton. Well, twelve years of that was enough!' He later studied English at Cambridge University and formed the hugely successful *Monty Python* team.

## John Peel

Radio presenter and journalist John Peel was born John Ravenscroft at Heswall Cottage Hospital and spent his formative years in the village of Burton. He was the longest-serving of the original BBC Radio 1 DJs, broadcasting regularly from 1967 until his death in 2004. His shows, including the Peel Sessions, helped bring bands such as The Undertones, The Smiths, Nirvana and The Fall to a wider audience. When once asked if he considered Liverpool to be his home, Peel showed his loyalty to Wirral in replying, 'No. I only said Liverpool to people at a later date because it was easier to say Liverpool than Burton, which is a small village on the edge of the river Dee where I lived until I was the age of 17.'

## Patricia Routledge

Katherine Patricia Routledge was born in Birkenhead in 1929 and educated at Mersey Park Primary School, and later Birkenhead High School. She went on to study English Literature and Language at the University of Liverpool, becoming involved in the institution's Drama Society. Her career in drama took her to stages across the globe, granting her fame both in musicals and television. She is best known for her role as Hyacinth Bucket in the series *Keeping Up Appearances*. In 2010 Patricia returned to Wirral to celebrate the fifth birthday of the St James Centre in Laird Street. 'It's very nice to be asked back and I love the Merseyside wit. It was wonderful on my ear when I visited the St James Centre. You're never done with your roots, even if you're on the other side of the world.'

## Ian Botham

Born in Heswall in 1955, Ian Botham carved out a remarkably successful career in the sport of cricket. He is generally regarded as being England's greatest ever all-rounder, particularly in Test cricket. Throughout his prolific career Botham broke a number of records, such as the first man to score a century and take 10 wickets in the same match, the youngest cricketer to take 200 Test wickets and the first player ever to reach 5,000 runs and 300 wickets. In 2007 Botham was knighted in recognition of his cricketing achievements and his continued efforts in raising money and publicity for leukaemia research. He is now an established commentator for Sky Sports and newspaper columnist.

## Daniel Craig

Chester-born actor Daniel Craig spent his formative years on the peninsula as a pupil at Holy Trinity Primary School in Hoylake and later Hilbre High School. Craig also completed a spell as a sixth former at Calday Grange Grammar School before moving to London to join the National Youth Theatre. He has since had roles in numerous films including *Lara Croft: Tomb Raider* with Angelina Jolie and *Road to Perdition* starring opposite Tom Hanks. However, his major breakthrough came along in 2006 when Craig was chosen to become the sixth actor to play James Bond in the film *Casino Royale*. Despite his A-list celebrity status he still remembers those back home and in 2012 urged support for a local cause close to his heart. 'People close to me have received treatment from the amazing staff at the Clatterbridge cancer centre, so I would urge everybody to do all they can to support their work.' He had previously supported the RNLI Hoylake Appeal, even penning a foreword for the visitors' brochure.

# Festivals

### The Wirral Food and Drink Festival

Every year food connoisseurs of the region are treated to a tantalising range of gastronomic delights. The festival often features exhibitors and stalls from the finest specialist food producers from all over the country with a veritable village of marquees and food courts. There is also live music and entertainment, brewery tents, celebrity chefs and various workshops teaching everything from cookery classes to circus skills. 2012 saw the festival's seventh appearance with over 20,000 attendees.

### The Wirral Egg Run

The Wirral Egg Run is world famous. The event began as 'The Wirral Easter Egg Run' in April 1981. It was a ride-out by New Brighton's Empress Motorcycle Club to Heswall's Children Hospital, with each rider taking an Easter egg gift for the patients. Back then about twenty riders took part, but the event has grown phenomenally since those early days with over 12,000 participants raising thousands of pounds for charity and good causes in 2012.

### The Wirral International Film Festival

This independent festival was the idea of Wirral producers Alan Veste and Phil Bimpson, who established the event in 2008. Its aim is to provide a showcase for the work of the borough's up and coming filmmakers and spread the word about the Wirral's artistic abilities. Over the years the event has gone from strength to strength, with screen enthusiasts entering very different and varied films covering a broad range of genres. The only criterion is that the entrant or their film must relate in some way to Wirral.

# WIRRAL
## FOOD&DRINK
# FESTIVAL

## The Scarecrow Festival

The Scarecrow Festival at Thornton Hough appears to have been too popular for its own good. It won the Mersey Tourism Award for Small Event of the Year in 2004 with the festival raising £75,000 for projects around the village. At its height the event drew crowds of over 35,000 but organisers struggled to cope with the mass influx. In 2010 Eastham hosted its own Scarecrow Festival attracting 2,000 visitors, but it is unknown whether either event will ever return.

## The Wirral Festival of Firsts

Germinating from an idea put forward by poet and former Scaffold member John Gorman, The Wirral Festival of Firsts has quickly captured the public imagination. It was originally established in Hoylake in 2011 in order to deliver an innovative community-based arts festival to encourage public participation and community cohesion. The festival provides a platform for showcasing local talent as well as the opportunity for the community to enjoy some of the best examples of art, music, poetry and theatre in the UK.

# Wirral in Days Gone By:
# Hamilton Square, Birkenhead

# Musicians

### The Coral

The Coral, who hail from Hoylake, formed in 1996 when schoolfriends Ian Skelly and Paul Duffy rehearsed together in the basement of the pub Flat Foot Sam's. The band first emerged onto the music scene during the early 2000s finding success with their self-titled debut album, *The Coral*, in 2002, followed by *Magic and Medicine*, in 2003. Their debut album was nominated for the 2002 Mercury Music Prize and later voted the fourth best album of the year by *NME Magazine*. In 2012 the band announced a hiatus in order to concentrate on individual projects but a seventh album is also rumoured to be in production.

### Half Man Half Biscuit

Half Man Half Biscuit have been active since the mid-1980s and are known for their satirical, sardonic and occasionally surreal songs. The band was formed when Birkenhead friends Neil Crossley and Nigel Blackwell grouped up with drummer Paul Wright and Nigel's guitarist brother, Simon. Their tracks were well received with their debut album *Back in the DHSS* reaching number one in the Indie Chart. They were often championed by DJ John Peel, for whom they recorded twelve sessions. In 2010 their track, 'Joy Division Oven Gloves' made it to No. 1 in the HMV UK Digital Downloads Top 40, knocking Ultravox's 'Vienna' from the top spot.

### Pete Burns

The eccentric singer Pete Burns, who made it famous with the band Dead or Alive, was born in Port Sunlight. He was the son of a German-Jewish refugee who had wed a British soldier. In an interview with the *Sunday Times*, Burns recalled how some children in the village had teased him because of his mother's German background. Nevertheless his distinctive personality thrived and he is now as famous for his unique outlandish style as much as his music. Burns's biggest hit was the 1985 track, 'You Spin Me Round (Like a Record)' which reached No.1 and remains a classic of British synth-pop.

## Elvis Costello

Declan MacManus, as he was then known, was born in London in 1954 to parents Lillian and Ronald. His Merseyside links are particularly strong. His mother was from Liverpool, his father Birkenhead and young Declan was actually christened at Holy Cross Church on Hoylake Road. By the time he was 17 years old his parents had divorced and he moved back to Wirral to live with his mother. It was here that he formed his first band, Rusty. Since then Costello has won multiple awards including a Grammy Award, and he has twice been nominated for the Brit Award for Best British Male. In 2003, Elvis Costello and the Attractions were inducted into the Rock and Roll Hall of Fame. The following year Rolling Stone ranked Costello number 80 on their list of the 100 Greatest Artists of All Time.

## Charlie Landsborough

One of the nation's best loved country stars is without doubt Charlie Landsborough. During the war his mother was evacuated to Wrexham to escape the bombing raids on the Birkenhead docklands which inevitably followed. His life would be a varied one, with Landsborough taking on a multitude of jobs ranging from telephone engineer, flour mill labourer, soldier and teacher. It was during his teaching profession that he penned his first major success, *What Colour is the Wind*, which became a huge hit in Ireland. Overall, sales of his albums have exceeded 700,000 with two No.1 singles in the Irish pop charts, and several of his albums topping the British country charts. *Still Can't Say Goodbye*, recorded in Nashville in 1999, saw Landsborough win the BMCA Best Male Vocalist in 2000, for the third year running, and the Southern Country Award for best album.

# Local Lingo

For those outside the area the Merseyside accent can be a little difficult to get to grips with. Some of the more unusual phrases locals may use are:

**Antwakky** – Old fashioned

**Beast** – Great

**Bevvie** – A drink

**On me Bill** – Alone

**Bizzies** – The police

**Chokka** – Very busy

**Class, Sound or Laughin** – Good or I like it

**Cob on** – To sulk or be unhappy

**Come ed** – Come on

**Deffo** – Certainly

**Divvy** – Stupid person

**Fit** – Attractive

**Geg** – To be nosy

**Happenin la?** – How are you?

**Iffy** – Strange

**Is right** – I agree

**Kecks** – Pants or underwear

**Kidda or La** – Friend

**Made up** – Pleased

**Messy** – Drunk

**No mark** – Someone of no importance

**Over the water** – Liverpool

**Scally** – Chav or mischievous character

**Scran** – Food

**Shady** – Unfair

**Us** – Me

**Woolyback** or **Plazzy Scouser** – A person from a town near to but not Liverpool itself

**Ya ma** – Your mother

**Youz** – You lot

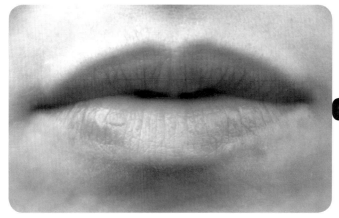

# Wirral on Screen

### Harry Potter and the Deathly Hallows Part 1

In September 2009 the Queensway Tunnel played host to a week of cinematic magic when a scene from the penultimate *Harry Potter* movie was filmed for the big screen. Recording took place during the night whilst the tunnel was closed for routine maintenance. Those fans eager to catch a glimpse of its star Daniel Radcliffe were most disappointed when it was discovered he was not personally involved in this particular shoot.

### Chariots of Fire

The Oval sports centre in Bebington was chosen to double up as Paris's Colombes stadium when film crews descended upon the town in 1981. The achievements of British runners Harold Abrahams and Eric Liddell, who had won the 100m and 400m events respectively, were depicted in this Oscar-winning blockbuster. Woodside Ferry terminal and the landing stage also featured, and was used to portray the port of Dover.

### Mike Bassett: England Manager

This satirical comedy saw Ricky Tomlinson become the fictional football manager Mike Bassett. The plot centres on Bassett's journey from running Norwich FC, to becoming head of the England team. The film resulted in a spin-off TV series which saw Tomlinson reprise his role to manage his boyhood club, Wirral County FC, with numerous scenes filmed on the peninsula.

### The Magnet

This 1950 flick sees a young Wallasey boy with a very rich imagination cheat a younger lad out of a magnet by offering him an invisible watch. *The Magnet* was filmed on location in and around New Brighton, Liverpool, and at Ealing Studios. Local accents, however, are absent until almost the end of the film in a scene filmed in the shadow of the Anglican cathedral. In 2012 the Light Cinema in New Brighton screened the movie after repeated requests from members of the public who remembered *The Magnet* being filmed.

### The 51st State

*The 51st State* is a 2001 Canadian-British action comedy film starring a host of well-known stars including Robert Carlyle, Rhys Ifans, Meat Loaf and Samuel L. Jackson. The film was almost entirely filmed in Merseyside, including Wirral's dockside areas with the East Float Mill featuring prominently.

PROD. NO.
SCENE
TAKE
ROLL
SOUND
DATE
PROD. CO.
DIRECTOR
CAMERAMAN

# Future Wirral

When Wirral Council gave its approval to Wirral Waters, it was giving the go-ahead to one of the UK's biggest ever regeneration plans. In a fifty-year scheme requiring £4.5 billion of investment, Wirral Waters is set to transform 500 acres of Birkenhead docklands into a go-to destination and create 27,000 new jobs. There will be five specially designed quarters – SkyCity, Northbank West, Northbank East, Marina View and Vittoria Studios, each filled with a variety of new developments. These buildings should not only help towards the regional and national economy, but will also give Wirral a waterfront to be proud of and a skyline dotted with skyscrapers and other towering constructions. The idea is highly ambitious but, if successful, this once neglected portion of the North West will be given a new lease of life and become an important location for residential, commercial and leisure opportunities for many.

The development team behind the process, Peel Holdings, are working with ten key goals in mind:

Celebrating the past, shaping the future

An internationally recognisable, city waterfront

Creating places of distinction, destinations and market concepts for the twenty-first century

A dynamic, prosperous Inner Wirral at the heart of the City Region

World-class connections, access for all

Sharing prosperity, health and well-being

An exemplar environmental resource

Securing long-term success, starting today

Engage and inspire

A robust delivery framework

Only time will tell if their exciting vision for Wirral will come to a successful fruition.

# Websites

www.visitwirral.com

www.wirral.gov.uk

www.wirralwaters.co.uk

www.wirralglobe.co.uk

www.wirraltalk.co.uk

www.wikiwirral.co.uk

www.spaceport.org.uk

www.portsunlightvillage.com

www.floralpavilion.com

www.tranmererovers.co.uk

# Things to do in Wirral

Take a leisurely stroll around Birkenhead Park and feed the ducks ☐

Treat yourself to a delicious ice-cream at Park Gate ☐

Grab your clubs for a game of pitch and putt in New Brighton ☐

Climb to the top of Bidston Hill and admire the gorgeous view ☐

Pick up a famous bar of Sunlight Soap at Port Sunlight museum ☐

Take to your saddle and explore Wirral's many picturesque cycle paths ☐

Head to Prenton Park for 90 minutes of electrifying football ☐

Investigate the historic salvaged U-Boat down at Woodside ☐

Visit the village of Thornton Hough and see the beautiful architecture ☐

Grab your bucket and spade and enjoy the sun at West Kirkby beach ☐

Have a drink or two at Heswall's fabulous selection of bars and pubs ☐

# Picture Credits:

Photographs are from the author's collection unless otherwise stated

3. Wirral's coat of arms
7. Merseyrail Stations; Wirral from Liverpool (Si Donbavand – www.flickr.com/xhupf)
9. The East Float Dock (Peter Craine); Leasowe Lighthouse (Sue Adair); Hoylake (Digitalurbanlandscape)
11. Map of Birkenhead dating from approximately 1900
12. A Punch and Judy puppet show, Thornton Hough (John Puddephatt)
13. New Brighton Lighthouse (Lukasz Lukomski)
15. A view of the American, Bridal Veil and Horseshoe Falls at Niagara Falls (Saffron Blaze); Temple Mount, Jerusalem (אסף.צ); Osaka Castle (663highland)
17. Landican Lane
19. New Brighton Beach, Wirral (Wikimedia Commons)
21. Tranmere Rovers at Prenton Park (Eric The Fish); The Boathouse, Parkgate; Conway Park Campus
23. Central Park, Liscard (Andrew D. Hurley)
25. Storm at New Brighton
27. Wirral Farmers Market; A Stena line vessel sails down the Mersey; The Floral Pavilion in New Brighton
29. A parent holds a child's hand (SanShoot); A sombre graveyard
31. A depiction of the sinking of HMS *Birkenhead* by Thomas M.M. Hemy in 1892; The sun goddess at Bidston Hill
33. The Wheatsheaf, Raby; A ferry sails towards Seacombe (calflier001)
35. A portrait of Daniel Defoe (THP)
37. A photograph of Nathaniel Hawthorne (LC-DIG-cwpbh-01082)
39. New Brighton funfair in its heyday
41. The grand entrance to Birkenhead Park (Barney Finlayson)
43. The entrance to the Lever Brothers factory in Port Sunlight
45. Michael Heseltine giving a speech in 2012 (bisgovuk); The Lever Building (Sweetie candykim)
47. Landing Stage, Woodside
49. A picture from the 3rd World Scout Jamboree held at Arrowe Park; The opening of the Queensway Tunnel
51. Torch bearer Ben Osu runs with the Olympic Flame (Ruth W)
53. Writing (SXC)
55. A page of the *Birkenhead and Cheshire Advertiser* from November 1880
57. Tranmere Police Division 1920 (www.liverpoolcitypolice.co.uk)

**59.** Students protest against the rising cost of education

**61.** A view of Hamilton Square and the Town Hall; The Lady Lever Art Gallery (Barney Finlayson)

**63.** Fort Perch Rock; Hadlow Road Station

**65.** The Asda superstore; The Concouse in West Kirkby; Part of the buildings in Civic Way, Bebington

**67.** Glasses... (SXC, credit:nkzs)

**69.** Beer (SXC)

**71.** Birkenhead Priory;Port Sunlight Village Museum; The U-Boat Story, Woodside; The Williamson Art Gallery (Barney Finlayson)

**73.** A leafy path in Arrowe Park; Ness Botanical Gardens

**75.** A 1915 advertisement for Cammell Laird

**77.** A photograph of Lord Lever

**79.** A photograph of F.E. Smith (LC-USZ62-45749)

**81.** Wirral Grammar School crest

**83.** An advertisement for the Hovercraft service from 1962; A sketch of the opening of Birkenhead Park, 1847; The Argyle Theatre, Argyle Street

**84.** Charing Cross, Birkenhead; Oxton Road Congregational Church

**85.** Central Park, Liscard; Little Sutton train station

**87.** The scene of George Fell's murder in Conway Street

**89.** News sketch of the details surrounding the murder of Nellie Clarke

**91.** The Bridge Inn, Port Sunlight (Barney Finlayson); Saint Andrews Church, Bebington

**93.** Scene of destruction in Manor Road, Wallasey; The bombed-out remains of a property in Oxton Road; An image showing what was left of Poulton Road Methodist Church, Wallasey

**95.** Wirral football legend Dixie Dean (Dr David France at en.wikipedia, CC-BY-SA-3.0)

**97.** Andrew Irvine

**99.** Microphone (SXC)

**101.** Record (SXC)

**103.** Daniel Craig (Caroline Bonarde Ucci)

**105.** Wirral Food and Drink Festival; Riders at the Wirral Egg Run

**107.** Organisers prepare for the Wirral Film Festival; Scarecrows laid out for the Scarecrow Festival

**109.** Hamilton Square, Birkenhead

**111.** Gig (SXC)

**113.** Holy Cross Church, Hoylake Road (Bas Hanrahan)

**115.** Lips (SXC)

**117.** The famous platform at King's Cross (Sachie Yamazaki, SXC)

**119.** Film Clapper (SXC)

**121.** An artist's impression of Wirral Waters

**123.** Laptop (SXC)

**125.** Windmill on Bidston Hill

Visit our website and discover thousands of
other History Press books.

**www.thehistorypress.co.uk**